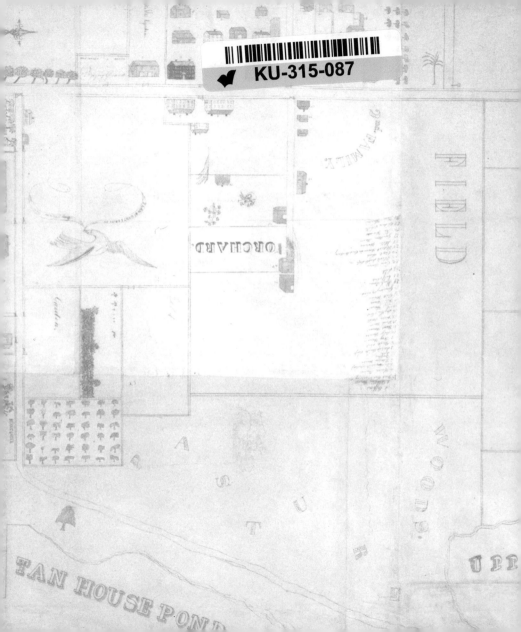

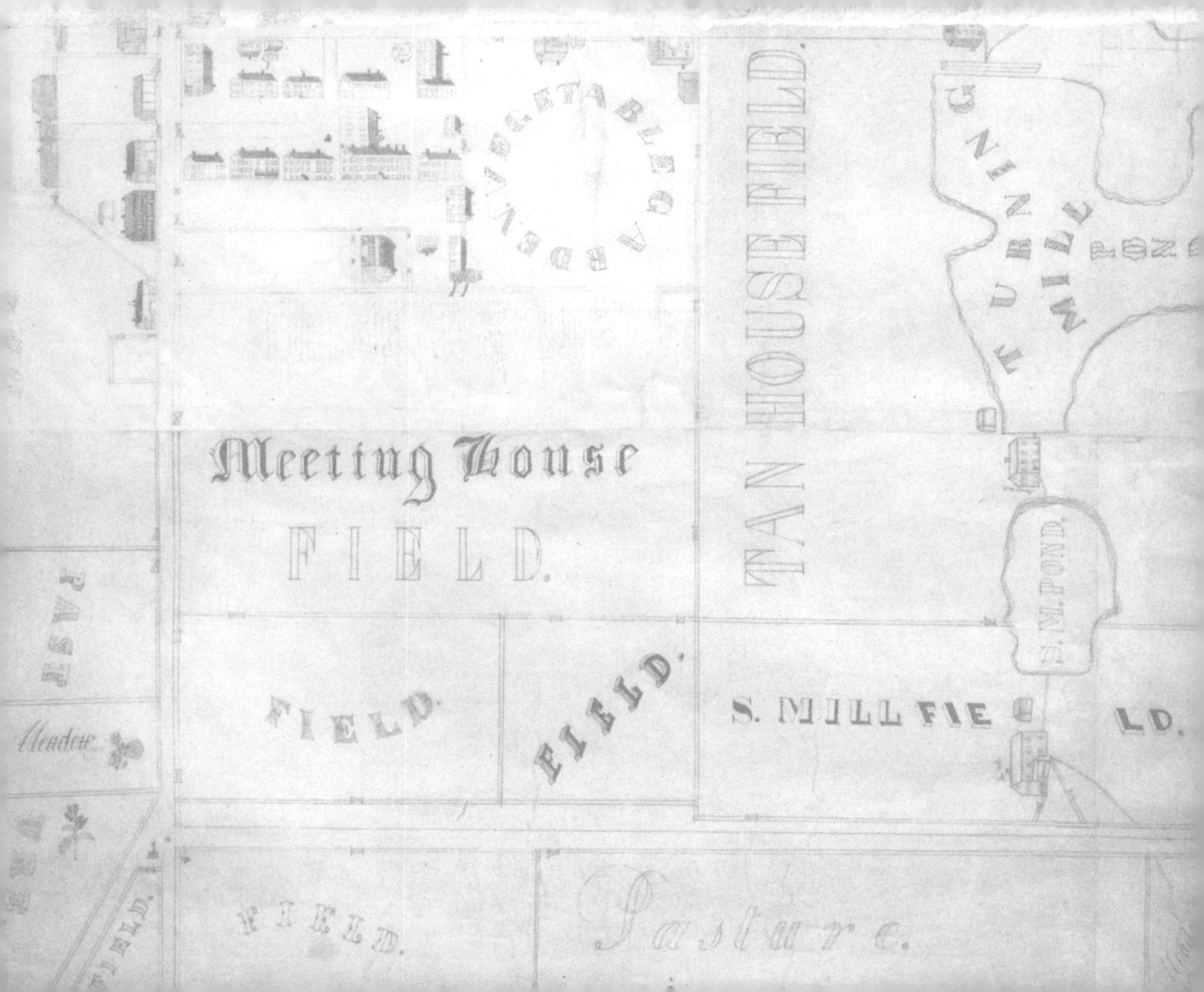

PAST

FIELD.

FIELD

FIELD.

FIELD.

Pasture

Meeting House

FIELD.

VEGETABLE GARDEN.

TAN HOUSE FIELD.

S. MILL FIELD

S. MILL FIELD.

S. M. POND.

TURNING

MILL

POND

WISDOM

from a

SHAKER

GARDEN

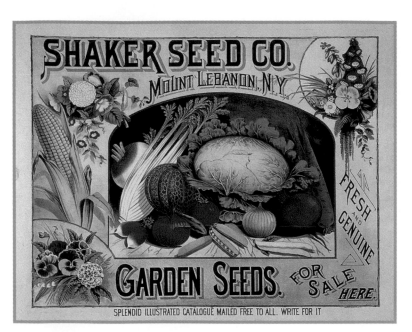

WISDOM

from a

SHAKER

GARDEN

KATHLEEN MAHONEY

PHOTOGRAPHS BY PAUL ROCHELEAU

PENGUIN STUDIO

Special thanks to Paul Rocheleau, Jerry Grant, Amy Bess Miller and Persis Fuller, Stephen and Miriam Miller, Mary-Ellen Weinrib, Cynthia Hunt, Marketa Sparrow, Larrie Curry, Sharon Koomler, Happy Griffith, Tommy Hines, Pei Koay, Elizabeth Kremer, Virginia McEwen, and Sarah Scheffel.

A special thank-you to the staff of the Shaker Village of Pleasant Hill in Harrodsburg, Kentucky, for its gracious hospitality.

—*K. M.*

PENGUIN STUDIO

Published by the Penguin Group

Penguin Putnam Inc., 375 Hudson Street, New York, New York 10014, U.S.A.

Penguin Books Ltd, 27 Wrights Lane, London W8 5TZ, England

Penguin Books Australia Ltd, Ringwood, Victoria, Australia

Penguin Books Canada Ltd, 10 Alcorn Avenue, Toronto, Ontario, Canada M4V 3B2

Penguin Books (N.Z.) Ltd, 182–190 Wairau Road, Auckland 10, New Zealand

Penguin Books Ltd, Registered Offices: Harmondsworth, Middlesex, England

First published in 1998 by Penguin Studio, a member of Penguin Putnam Inc.

1 3 5 7 9 10 8 6 4 2

ISBN 0–670–87365–9

CIP data available.

A NOTE TO THE READER: This book contains information on herbs, the use of which may cause an allergic reaction in some individuals. Before using any herbal remedy first sample a small quantity to determine if you have any adverse or allergic reaction. Neither the author nor the publisher is responsible for any adverse effects or consequences resulting from the use of the formulas or other information contained herein.

Printed in Singapore

Designed by Pei Koay

Contents

Introduction

From the moment the early Shakers set down roots in America, in the 1700s, nature played a vital role in their existence. With agriculture the mainstay of the Shakers' economy throughout much of the nineteenth century, vast expanses of farmland, distinguished by a sense of harmony and order, were an integral part of their communities.

Shaker gardens and orchards included a wide range of vegetables and fruits as well as herbs and flowers. They also cultivated physics gardens, where they grew their medicinal plants, for use in their industries. The cultivation of land brought economic security, but the rewards went well beyond that. Nature lent inspiration to the simple spirit of the Shakers, appealing to their senses and influencing their thoughts. They frequently turned to the imagery of nature in their heartfelt writings as well as in their lovely spirit drawings.

A small group of eight Shakers, under the leadership of Mother Ann Lee, originally arrived in America shortly before the

American Revolution, having left England in search of religious freedom. The sect, formally named the United Society of Believers in Christ's Second Appearing, was to reach its zenith around the middle of the nineteenth century, when membership climbed to close to five thousand. Communities were formed as soon as it was financially feasible. Personal possessions were relinquished. Through hard work and celibacy, they committed their lives totally to God.

Shaker doctrine advocated separation from the world; this isolation, however, did not extend to economic matters. Innovative as well as industrious, the Shakers had a genius for organization. Many of their industries, initially started to meet the communities' needs, were tied to the soil. Always striving toward perfection, they constantly experimented to improve the quality of their produce as they kept up with the latest in farming through books and journals, readily adopting new practices and improved labor-saving devices.

The New Lebanon and Watervliet communities were the first to sell garden seeds; by 1800, all of the communities then in existence had a thriving seed business in place. Of their many commercial enterprises, this proved to be the best known and the most profitable. Its success was the result of the high germination count of the seeds as well as the Shakers' reputation for fair dealing.

Seeds were first sold by Shaker peddlers and merchants. Later,

Shaker boxes filled with up to two hundred neat paper packets of seeds, each selling for around five cents, sat on counters in hardware and general stores accompanied by brightly colored posters advertising them.

With the construction of the Erie Canal and the completion of railroads that linked the country, Shaker seeds began being shipped throughout the nation. By mid-century, New Lebanon offered ninety varieties of vegetable and fruit seeds. Competition from outside companies became fierce after the Civil War, forcing this community to change its plain brown envelopes to colored ones with inviting illustrations.

By the 1830s, communities had started distributing seed catalogs; in 1835 New Lebanon issued *The Gardener's Manual,* with a second edition in 1843. The booklet provided helpful directions on selecting, preparing, and managing a kitchen garden. It covered an assortment of topics from pest control to preserving vegetables in winter as well as their uses, cooking instructions, and pickling. The purpose of the manual was to enable their dealers "to afford instructions, at a trifling expense, [to their] customers [who] may wish to obtain practical information relative to the raising and management of those valuable kitchen vegetables which are considered the most useful and important in a family."

Early Shakers were the first in the United States to cultivate a variety of herbs, roots, bark, and vegetable extracts on a major scale for physicians and druggists. At first, their main source for medicinals was wild herbs. *The Shaker Manifesto,* the Society's official publication, records 1820 as the start of sales of Shaker herbs and roots although they had been harvesting medicinal plants for their own use twenty years earlier. New Lebanon, with over fifty acres of land cultivated for a physics garden, was the first community to offer herbs, roots, and extracts for sale. As business grew, the Shakers started to cultivate most of their own plants in addition to purchasing produce from growers outside the community.

Many drugs on the market were of questionable quality, but the Shaker brand name printed on a product signified the highest quality at a time when few standards existed. By 1831, the reputation of Shaker medicinals had spread far and wide, with orders coming in from as far away as Europe. In 1852, the members pressed forty-two thousand pounds of roots, herbs, and bark. Other communities such as Canterbury and Enfield, New Hampshire; Harvard, Massachusetts; and Union Village, Ohio, also had significant herb businesses.

Several communities developed medicinal preparations. Some were produced by the Shakers and marketed by outside companies. Others, like Tincture of Veratrum Viride, were manufactured by the Shakers for physicians. Medicinal remedies produced by the Shakers, with such names as Corbett's Shaker Syrup of Sarsaparilla, Corbett's Wild Cherry Pectoral Syrup, Sanford's Radical

Cure, and Shakers' Aromatic Elixir of Malt, promised relief from a wide assortment of ailments that ranged from asthma, constipation, dyspepsia, loss of breath, and bad breath to disorders of the liver and kidneys. They were touted as being valuable for "regulating, purifying and invigorating the female functions" and for restoring the appetite and enriching the blood. The alcoholic content of most tonics was high.

A Shaker catalog printed just before the Civil War listed 354 assortments of medicinal and culinary plants, roots, bark, berries, seeds, and flowers. These were dried, pulverized, distilled, and condensed, then turned into powders, ointments, tinctures, lotions, pills, syrups, extracts, oils, and fragrant waters. At one time, most of the medicinal opium made in the United States was produced by the Shakers.

Good cooks were highly regarded by the Shakers, who thoroughly enjoyed hearty meals. With abundant orchards that included peach, damson plum, cherry, quince, and apple trees, and smaller fruits such as strawberries, raspberries, blackberries, gooseberries, currants, and grapes, a plentiful supply of preserves was put up to last the community throughout the winter months. According to the *Shaker's Farm Annual* (South Union, Kentucky, 1885), "Visitors to the village invariably appreciated the excellence of the article, claiming that Shaker Preserves were unrivaled in flavor and purity. By this means our Preserves acquired quite a local reputation. It occurred to the then Trustee that our surplus might be disposed of by sale. On making the experiment he was astonished and delighted to find that they met with ready sale and commanded the highest figures in the local markets."

Men worked the heavy machinery; many of the women were occupied in what were called household industries, preparing a wide variety of edible products for sale, including jellies and preserves, maple syrup and sugar, dried apples and sweet corn, applesauce and tomato sauce, catsup, pickles and relishes, and wine. Rosewater was sold both as a perfume and as a flavoring for apple pies. In 1860, thirty-five tons of jellies and preserves were sold at Pleasant Hill, Kentucky, alone. Apples were pressed into hard cider and brandy; grapes were made into wine. Distilling began around 1823, but, five years later, the parent ministry frowned upon the use of "ardent spirits" except in medicinal remedies.

After the Civil War, with the Industrial Revolution well under way, the country turned from agriculture to commerce. Many of the male Shakers abandoned the communities for work in the cities. There were not enough men left to operate the Shakers' labor-intensive industries nor were they able to be competitive in their pricing. By the late 1880s, the seed business came to an end. The herb industry lingered for another ten or so years before it too folded. Yet this tradition of farming lives on into the twentieth century. The handful of Shakers at the sole surviving community in

Maine have again started to reap the rewards found in working the land, producing an assortment of herbs for sale.

The Shakers' songs and poetry, filled with the abundance of nature that enriched their lives, also continue to endure. We can find pleasure and a sense of contentment in the simple writings their gardens inspired.

A Bountiful Garden

THE

GARDENER'S MANUAL;

CONTAINING

PLAIN INSTRUCTIONS FOR THE SELECTION, PREPARATION, AND

MANAGEMENT OF A

KITCHEN GARDEN:

WITH PRACTICAL DIRECTIONS FOR THE CULTI-

VATION AND MANAGEMENT OF SOME

OF THE MOST USEFUL

CULINARY VEGETABLES.

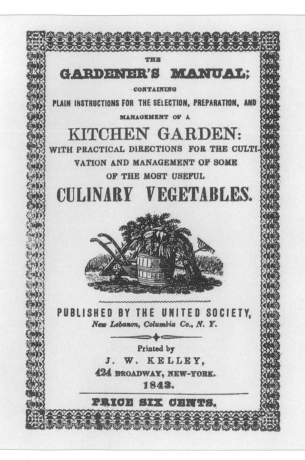

PUBLISHED BY THE UNITED SOCIETY,

New Lebanon, Columbia Co., N. Y.

Printed by

J. W. KELLEY,

424 BROADWAY, NEW-YORK.

1843.

PRICE SIX CENTS.

Successful agriculture calls for something more than mere application of sinew. It is not enough to plant and hoe. Intellectual must mingle with physical toil—a good head, as well as a strong arm, is required.

> — *The Farmer's Second Book*
> James Holmes, 1853

If you would have a lovely garden,
you should have a lovely life.
— *The Gardener's Manual*, 1843

The garden is said to be an index of the owner's mind. If this be true, many who otherwise might be acquitted, must be judged to possess minds susceptible of much improvement in order, usefulness, and beauty. A well prepared and a well cultivated garden is as much superior to a neglected one as, doubtless many who love idleness even better than they love themselves will be slow to admit.

> — *The Gardener's Manual*, 1843

Directions for the Selection of a Garden Spot

Situation. In choosing a site for a garden, a spot of even land, slightly inclining to the south or east, and having the full benefit of sun, is to be preferred. It should be situated near the dwelling, and neatly enclosed with a high wall, or a tight board fence.

Soil. Deep, dry, light, and rich, are the essential requisites of a good garden soil; and if not so naturally, it should be made so by art. If wet, draining should be resorted to; if too shallow, deep ploughing; if poor, manuring; if stony, they should be got off; — and thus should every impediment and obstruction to a good sweet soil, be reversed or removed by industry and art.

Size. The shape of a garden should be either square or oblong, both for convenience and looks.

— *The Gardener's Manual,* 1843

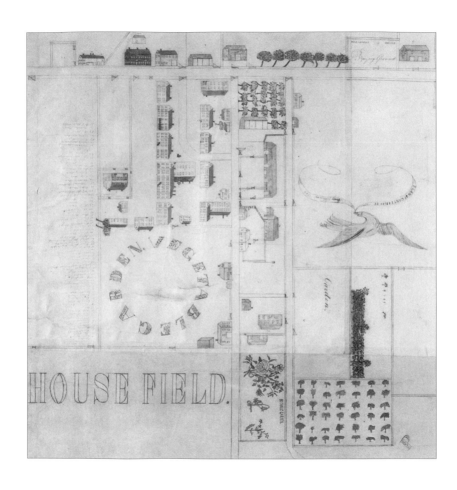

HOUSE FIELD.

Love, consolation, and peace bloom only
in the garden of sweet contentment.
— Martha J. Anderson, Mt. Lebanon, New York

Seeds

Thou who knowest all our weakness,
Leave us not to sow alone!
Bid thine angels guard the furrows,
Where the precious grain is sown;
Till the fields are crowned with glory;
Filled with mellow, ripened ears —
Filled with fruit of life eternal,
From the seed we sowed in tears.
— Song verse from *The Shaker Manifesto,* 1879

Of Preparing the Ground

Let it be stated, once for all, that all culinary vegetables do best upon a good rich soil; therefore let your land, if not naturally quite rich, be plentifully manured.

The best manure for a garden is a compost, of one part mineral substances, as ashes, lime, sand or clay, (as the soil may require), salt, &c.: five parts vegetable matter, as weeds, straw, leaves, roots and stalks of plants, and tan bark or sawdust to make the soil light, if necessary; and six parts of animal excrement. These should be collected in the course of the season, and mixed well together, to cause them to ferment. In the fall, this compost should be spread evenly upon the garden, and ploughed in.

— *The Gardener's Manual*, 1843

Beautiful Home

We are sowing, daily sowing
Seed, in future fruit to bear;
Shall the harvest bring us blessing
Or yield us anxious care?
Heaven guide us, Angel aid us
As we work we'll watch and pray
Thus we'll scatter seeds of goodness
To blossom in another's way.
—Song from *Hymns and Anthems in the Hour of Worship*
    Canterbury, New Hampshire, 1872

You might as well plant the seeds of noxious weeds,
and expect them not to grow, as to cherish
"little vices" and not calculate on their increase.
—Daniel Orcutt, Enfield, Connecticut

Putting in Crops

Sowing. If the seeds are to be planted out in open air this should not be done until the ground is sufficiently warm. . . . Seeds should never be sown broadcast, but in drills, so as to admit the requisite supply of light and air, and to allow the free use of the hoe. Cover with fine dirt, and not too deep, or the seed will rot before vegetating. Care must be taken to prevent the ground from forming a crust over the seeds, or becoming too dry while the plant is coming up.

—Descriptive Catalogue of Vegetable Seeds,
Raised at New Lebanon, New York, 1873

Some people at farming and gardening have skill,
And know how to plow well, to plant and to till;
But this is not all that a good farmer needs,
He ought to have judgment in buying good seeds.
For planting poor seeds did never yet pay,
The labor expended is time thrown away.

—Rural Register and Almanac for 1876
Mt. Lebanon, New York

The Beauties of Nature

The beauties of nature are charming to me
I love to behold their delights
The fields and the meadows & tall forest trees
Oh! Oh! What a beautiful sight.

The dark silent groves the vines and sweet flowers
The valley and low murmuring stream
All speak of Jehovah this Almighty power
In every direction is seen.

The broad face of nature is smiling on us
Just listen to the songsters so gay
They warble God's praise in their sweet wood notes wild
Throughout the bright summer days.

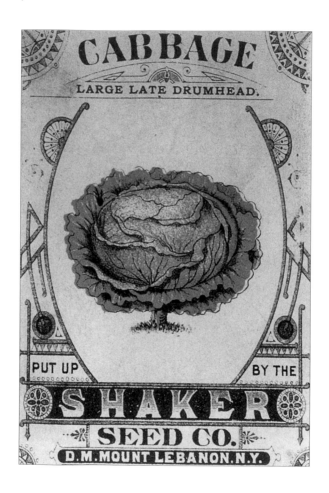

Go work with ardent courage,
And sow with willing hand
The seed o'er barren deserts,
And o'er the fertile land.

And, lo! earth yet shall blossom,
Though the brighter morn delays;
For God perfects the harvest,
Yea, "after many days."
—*Mother Ann Lee*
    Elder Henry Clay Blinn
    Canterbury, New Hampshire

Vanity is a fruitful soil for every evil plant.
—*Dew Drops of Wisdom*
    Elder Henry Clay Blinn
    Canterbury, New Hampshire

Selfishness blights the growth of every virtue.
—Martha J. Anderson, Mt. Lebanon, New York

May

The seed now buried in the earth
Will soon spring up and smile
Adding charms to pleasant mirth
And bless the farmer's toil.
—Shaker journal in the Western Reserve Library

The happiness of our whole life depends
on the cultivation of a good disposition.
—Alice Chadwick, Enfield, Connecticut

Of Cultivation

Weeds. Ah! here are our old friends again. But we cannot afford to keep them though there is a world of beauty in each. Like all living things, they seek to perpetuate their kind, and will deposit countless thousands of their minute seeds to make sure a future crop. Faithful constant hoeing only will prevent their being in the ascendant.

— The Farmer's Second Book
Sabbathday Lake, Maine, 1853

Hoeing should be performed as soon as the plants are fairly up, and continued as often as necessary. Thinning may be performed, the first time as soon as the plants are fairly in sight, the second after they are large enough to show which will make thrifty plants. Leaving plants too thick is a prevalent error, and one to which gardeners are very liable.

— The Gardener's Manual, 1843

> Say not to thy friend, there are weeds
> in your garden, when thy own is choked
> with the same; but rather look at home.
> *— Youth's Guide in Zion*

Never slacken your hand
in cultivating the good soil
of the heart; carefully guard
the good plants, and water them
with charity and love, which will be
like the refreshing dews.
— Hannah Potter, Mt. Lebanon, New York

Plough deep the fallow ground of the heart;
sow and cultivate the seeds of purity, love,
and truth, and you will reap a rich harvest
of true felicity.
— D. Austin Buckingham, Watervliet, New York

Thanksgiving

Bless'd by the sunshine and the showers,
Earth yields her fruitage and her flowers,
Thank offering unto God.
The golden grain and precious ores
She gives from out her treasures stores
As labor's rich reward.

Thus in our hearts, faith's choicest seed,
Well cultured without tare or weed,
Will flourish and increase.
And buds of heav'nly purity
Will bloom to full maturity,
With ripened fruits of peace.
—Original Shaker Music
    North Family of Mt. Lebanon, New York, 1893

Health. Do not be tempted to over-exertion. Drink sparingly of cold water when heated. Retire early, and rise early, and while you labor in the cool of the morning listen to the new voices about you; the bittern in the meadow, calling to his faithful mate in notes not unlike the noise made by pumping; the lark whistling on the topmost twig of the old apple tree, and the numerous other voices peculiar to the fresh and delightful hour.

— The Farmer's Second Book
James Holmes, 1853

We would like to say to our many friends who are engaged in cultivating the soil, we wish you much prosperity in this the most honorable, and at the same time, the most pleasantest, of all vocations.

— Descriptive Catalogue of Vegetable Seeds,
Raised at New Lebanon, New York, 1873

Medicinal Plants

and Remedies

Behold the Flowers that deck the Field,
The Gentle breeze perfuming,
And Tender Herbs their Fragrance Yield
Are Health and Life Defusing.
—From an herb catalog
Harvard Community, Massachusetts, 1843

A blade of grass—a simple flower,
Cull'd from the dewy lea;
These, these shall speak, with touching power,
Of change and health to thee.
—*Catalogue of Medicinal Plants, Barks,*
Roots, Seeds, Flowers and Select Powders
New Lebanon, New York, 1833

Why send to Europe's distant shores
For plants which grow at our own doors?
—From an herb catalog, 1833

A Sampling of Medicinal Plants

Angelica, leaves, root, seed
Biennial, sow seeds late summer, fall
Digestive tonic, stimulates appetite, good for respiratory problems

Chamomile, flowers
Perennial, sow seeds or plant divisions in early spring
Tonic for poor appetite, reduces fever, settles stomach, mild sedative, relieves menstrual pain

Comfrey, leaves, root
Perennial, plant divisions in spring and fall
External: skin softener, poultice for cuts and bruises, ulcerations and rheumatism

Coriander, seed
Annual, sow seed in spring
Expels intestinal gas, strengthens stomach, digestive for colic, mild sedative. External: poultice to relieve pain in joints

Dandelion, leaves and root

Perennial, seeds spread in fall

Tonic, corrects bilious secretions, aids liver and kidney problems, mild laxative. External: astringent

Dill, seed

Annual, sow seeds in spring

Expels intestinal gas, strengthens stomach, sedative, increases lactation

Fennel, leaves, seed

Perennial or biennial, sow seed in fall

Mild sedative, expels intestinal gas, strengthens stomach, a diuretic, allays hunger—good for weight loss. External: eye wash

Feverfew, flowers, leaves

Perennial, sow seeds or plant divisions and cuttings in spring or fall

Good for migraines, strengthens nerves and stomach, reduces inflammation in arthritic joints. External: moth repellent

Garlick, cloves

Perennial or biennial, plant cloves spring or fall

Stimulant, promotes discharge from the lungs, good for colds, bronchitis and dysentery, a diuretic, good for hypertension. External: controls dandruff, relieves rheumatism, an antiseptic

Golden Seal, leaves, root

Perennial, divide roots

Tonic, good for colds and bronchitis, relieves mouth sores and bladder infection

Lavender, flowers

Perennial shrub, sow seeds late spring or plant cuttings and divisions in spring or late summer

Strengthens nerves, expels intestinal gas, beneficial in diseases of the chest, helps relieve nausea, sedative. External: antiseptic, poultice relieves sprains, repels insects

Lemon Balm, leaves

Perennial, sow seeds or plant divisions and stem cuttings spring or fall

Strengthens stomach, produces perspiration, reduces fever, calms nerves, induces sleep, dispels melancholy. External: eases insect bites

Marigold, flowers, leaves

Perennial and annual, sow seeds or plant cuttings and divisions in spring

Strengthens the stomach. External: heals wounds, leaves good for bee stings, pest repellent

Nettle, leaves

Perennial, sow seeds or divide roots in spring

Digestive tonic, relief of rheumatism, good diuretic, lowers blood pressure. External: astringent, prevents dandruff, relieves eczema

Rosemary, flowers, leaves

Perennial shrub, plant cuttings or divide roots late spring

Tonic, diuretic, for colds, coughs, headaches. External: astringent, insect repellent

Sage, leaves

Perennial shrub, plant cuttings or divide roots in spring

Produces perspiration, strengthens stomach, aids digestion. External: antiseptic, for mouth sores and sore throat, strengthens gums

Sweet Basil, leaves

Annual, sow seeds and plant cuttings spring

Stimulant, relieves stomach ache, headache and spasms, stops vomiting. External: repels flies and mosquitoes

Tansy, flowers, leaves

Perennial, sow seeds or divide roots in spring and fall

External: repels insects

Valerian, root

Perennial, sow seeds or divide roots in spring and fall

Mild tranquilizer and sedative (use in moderation), good for insomnia and migraine

Yarrow, leaves

Perennial, sow seeds or divide roots in spring or fall

Relieves dysentery, alleviates toothaches, reduces fever and colds, strengthens stomach, diuretic. External: astringent

A Remedy for the Season

A lump of wet saleratus [baking soda], applied to the sting of a wasp or bee, will stop the pain in one moment, and prevent it from swelling.

—*The Farmer's Second Book*
Sabbathday Lake, Maine, 1853

Fly Banishment

It is freely circulated, that the combined odors of a geranium and calceolaria in any room, will effectually banish flies.

—*The Shaker Manifesto*, vol. 9
August 1879

Hair Restorative

Put ½ lb. pulv. Lobelia herb in bottle, add to it equal parts of Whisky, Brandy and olive oil. Bathe the head once a day, it will prevent the loss of hair and is said to restore it.

—Groveland, New York

Evening Confirmation

The faithful soul finds comfort
In meekness and repose,
His paths are strew'd with flowers,
The lily and the rose;
Their branches, far extending,
Perfume the fragrant air;
Lord, make me a partaker,
Through humbleness and prayer.
—Song from the *Collection of Millennial Hymns,*
Adopted to the Present Order of the Church
Canterbury, New Hampshire, 1847

Receipt for a regulating Cyrip

Take of the following barks one pound each—Poplar Cherry, Quaking ash and Butternut. These are to be boiled in twelve gallons of water for twelve hours. Strain and add four pounds of sugar and boil down to one gallon—then, add one quart of Rum. Dose to be taken two tablespoons full an hour before eating breakfast and two an hour before eating dinner. It is preferable to use the barks while green.

—For Eldress Betsy Bates

Asenath Edie, Union Village, Ohio

The humble and wise who strive
to keep their virtues in disguise
are like the beautiful blossoms
which send forth their rich perfume
long before their beauty is seen.
— Mabel Lane
    Mt. Lebanon, New York

Ill will, like the blighting frost,
destroys life's sweetest blossoms.
— Martha Anderson
    Mt. Lebanon, New York

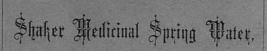

Good wines possess highly valuable and restorative medicinal . . . properties for refreshing and supporting the sick. They cheer and enliven the spirits of the weak and feeble and give strength and comfort both to the mind and body.

—Groveland, New York

Remember, if water source is doubtful, drink the wine.

—Old Chatham Museum manuscript

To Get the Oil of Roses

Take a large jar and fill it clean with flowers of roses. Cover them with pure water & set it in the sun in the day time & take in at night for 7 days when the oil will float on the top. Take this off with some cotten tied on a stick and squeeze in a phyal & stop it up close.

—Old Shaker journal

Perfume and Preventative of Moths

Take of cloves, caraway seeds, nutmegs, mace, cinnamon and sanguin (blood root) beans of each one ounce: Then add as much Florentine orris root as will equal the other ingredients put together. Grind the whole well to pouder, & then put it in little bags among your clothes.

—Old Shaker journal

Purest Blessing

Shun the thorn and grow the flower,
Speak no sentiment unkind;
Let thy life like balmy showers,
Give sweet fragrance to the mind.
For with days so swiftly passing,
Friends may go and come no more;
Let them bear thy purest blessing,
Giving but refills thy store.
—Song from *Hymns and Anthems in the Hour of Worship*
　Canterbury, New Hampshire, 1872

If every good deed and kindly thought here,
formed a flower in the pathway beyond,
how beautiful, how rich in sweet perfume
must be the way up the hill to God.
—Daniel Orcutt
　Enfield, Connecticut

The Shaker Pantry

If talent, genius and skill are looking for a good missionary field, the kitchen is the great uncivilized realm.

— *The Shaker Manifesto,* 1883

Shaker Lemon Pie

2 large lemons
4 eggs, well beaten
2 cups sugar

Slice lemons as thin as paper, rind and all. Combine with sugar; mix well. Let stand 2 hours or longer, preferably blending occasionally. Add beaten eggs to lemon mixture; mix well. Turn into nine inch pie shell, arranging lemon slices evenly. Cover with top crust. Cut several slits near center. Bake at 450°F for 15 minutes. Reduce heat to 375°F and bake for about 20 minutes or until silver knife inserted near edge of pie comes out clean. Cool before serving.

— *We Make You Kindly Welcome*
Elizabeth Kremer, 1970
Pleasant Hill, Kentucky

No cook is really good without a lively imagination and the will to use it.

—Sister Lisset, North Union, Ohio

Good fruit is desirable at breakfast. It has been said that in the morning it is gold, at noon silver and at night lead.

—*Mary Whitcher's Shaker House-Keeper,* 1882

Fruit may be preserved with honey by putting the fruit first in the can, then pouring honey over it, and seal air-tight; when the honey is poured from the fruit it will have the flavor and appearance of jelly, making a delicious dessert.

—*The Shaker Manifesto,* 1882

SHAKER APPLE SAUCE

Address **D. C. BRAINARD**, ···· PACKED AT ···· MT. LEBANON, COL., CO., N. Y.

FRESH APPLES

Address: **D. C. BRAINARD & CO.**, Mt. Lebanon, Col. Co., N. Y.

SHAKER FRUIT

PACKED AT

MOUNT LEBANON

COLUMBIA CO.,

N. Y.

Tomato or Love Apple

This is a very healthy vegetable, and a great favorite when we become accustomed to it, though generally not very palatable at first.

— The Gardener's Manual, 1843

Shaker Tomato Jam
Hancock, Massachusetts

4 pounds ripe tomatoes

16 cups sugar

4 large oranges

8 lemons

3 sticks cinnamon

Scald tomatoes to remove skins and chop fine. Add sugar, the juice and grated rind of oranges and lemons, and cinnamon and cook until it jells on spoon. Skim, pour into sterilized jars, and seal. Makes 4 to 5 pints.

— The Best of Shaker Cooking
Amy Bess Miller and
Persis Fuller, 1985

Amelia's Sour Cherry Jam
North Union, Ohio

$\frac{1}{2}$ cup cracked cherry pits

16 cups (4 quarts) pitted sour cherries

12 cups (3 quarts) white sugar

Add cracked pits tied in cheesecloth to the pitted cherries and sugar. Cook together for $1\frac{1}{2}$ hours, or until the jam thickens and the cherries take on a dark color. Remove bag of pits and pour jam into scalded sterilized jars and seal. Makes 6 to 8 pints.

> — *The Best of Shaker Cooking*
> Amy Bess Miller and
> Persis Fuller, 1985

To Pickle Peaches

Take a half bushel of peaches, rub them clean with a flannel cloth, then stick into each one four cloves.

Take 1 gallon of vinegar, 1 quart of molasses, and 2 pounds sugar. Heat all together. When scalding hot, put in the peaches and let them simmer a few minutes. Then put all in a jar. After standing nine or ten days, remove the peaches from the liquid, scald it and pour it over the peaches, and put up in such jars as you choose; glass is best.

— Old Shaker journal

Raspberry Vinegar

To two quarts of raspberries put one pint of cider vinegar. After two or three days mash the fruit and strain through a bag. To every pint allow a pound of sugar. Boil twenty minutes and skim. Bottle when cold. Makes a pleasant drink put into water.

— *Mary Whitcher's Shaker House-Keeper,* 1882

Shaker Wheaten Bread

1 cup milk	1 cake yeast
1 tablespoon salt	1 cup warm water
3 tablespoons butter	4 cups sifted flour
4 tablespoons honey or maple syrup	4 cups whole wheat flour

Scald milk; add salt, butter, syrup and ¾ cup of warm water; stir well. Let cool to lukewarm. In the remaining ¼ cup water dissolve the yeast; add to other mixture. Add flours gradually and knead into a smooth ball. Place in buttered bowl and brush top with soft butter. Let rise to double its bulk. Knead lightly this time and shape into loaf. Again brush with soft butter and let rise to twice its bulk. Bake at 350°F for 50 to 60 minutes.

> — *We Make You Kindly Welcome*
> Elizabeth Kremer, 1970
> Pleasant Hill, Kentucky

Give the stomach good, wholesome food, and it will fill your veins with pure blood, which in turn will give you a healthy brain and drive away the whole brood of manufactured troubles.

> — *The Shaker Manifesto*, 1883

Beets and carrots should be gathered before hard frosts in the fall, the tops cut off and the roots packed away in sand in a warm cellar. Onions and turnips keep well on scaffolds or in barrels in a dry cool cellar.

— *The Gardener's Manual,* 1843

How to Tell a Good Potato

These are the requisite qualities for a good potato when one is cut in two; there must be a considerable amount of moisture, though not too much; rub the two pieces together and a white froth will appear; this signifies the presence of starch, and the more starch, the better the potato.

— *The Shaker Manifesto,* 1881

Make no show of taking great delight in your victuals, feed not with greediness; lean not on the table, neither find fault with what you eat.

—*A Juvenile Guide, or Manual of*
Good Manners
Canterbury, New Hampshire, 1844

Potatoes, cabbage, turnip, beet,
And every kind of thing you eat,
Must neatly on your plate be laid,
Before you eat with pliant blade:
Nor ever — 'tis an awkward matter,
To eat or sip out of the platter.

When bread or pie you cut or break,
Touch only what you mean to take;
And have no prints of fingers seen
On that that's left — nay, if they're clean.

—*Advice to Children on Behavior at Table*
A nineteenth-century Shaker poem

Sweet Corn Fritters

1 pint (2 cups) soaked corn

½ cup milk

½ cup flour

3 tablespoons melted butter

½ teaspoon black pepper

½ teaspoon salt

1 egg

Beat and mix all together. Cook as griddle cakes. An excellent style of using it.

—*Mary Whitcher's Shaker*
House-Keeper, 1882

Corn by the common usage is eaten from the cob, but the exhibition is not interesting.

—*Gentle Manners*
East Canterbury,
New Hampshire, 1899

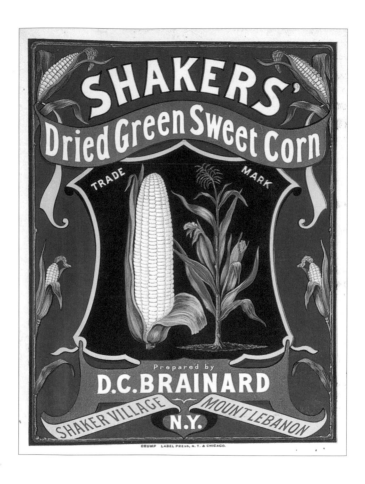

Corn Relish

Hancock, Massachusetts

4 cups skinned and chopped onions

4 cups peeled and chopped ripe tomatoes

4 cups peeled and chopped cucumbers

4 cups corn cut from cob

4 cups chopped cabbage

4 cups sugar

1 tablespoon salt

1 tablespoon celery seeds

1 teaspoon turmeric

4 cups vinegar

Mix vegetables together in large saucepan. Add remaining ingredients and bring to boil. Reduce heat and simmer 20 minutes uncovered. Put into sterilized glass containers; seal. Makes two quarts.

> —*The Best of Shaker Cooking*
> Amy Bess Miller and
> Persis Fuller, 1985

Pumpkin Muffins

$3/4$ cup brown sugar

$1/4$ cup molasses

$1/2$ cup soft butter

1 beaten egg

$1/4$ cup pecans

1 cup cooked mashed pumpkin

1 teaspoon baking soda

$1/4$ teaspoon salt

$1\,3/4$ cups flour

Cook, drain and mash pumpkin; put through strainer. Cream sugar, molasses and butter; add egg and pumpkin and blend well. Mix the flour with baking soda and salt. Beat mixture into the pumpkin batter. Fold in pecans. Fill well-greased muffin pans about $1/2$ full with batter. Bake at 375° for 20 minutes. Makes $1\,1/4$ dozen muffins.

— *We Make You Kindly Welcome*
Elizabeth Kremer, 1970
Pleasant Hill, Kentucky

Shaker Boiled Apples

About the nicest morsel that ever tickled the palate is a boiled apple; not boiled like a potato nor steamed like a dumpling, but as follows: Place a layer of fair-skinned Baldwins, or any other nice varieties, in a stew-pan, with about a quarter of an inch of water. Throw on about half a cup of sugar to six good-sized apples, and boil until the apples are thoroughly cooked and the syrup nearly thick enough for jelly. After one trial no one would, for any consideration, have fair-skinned apples peeled. The skins contain a very large share of the jelly-making substance, and impart a flavor impossible to obtain otherwise.

—Mary Whitcher's Shaker
House-Keeper, 1882

Inhale the fresh air freely before partaking of the morning meal, it gives zest to it.

—The Shaker Manifesto, 1878

Bibliography

Andrews, Edward Deming, and Faith Andrews. *Fruits of the Shaker Tree of Life: Memoirs of Fifty Years of Collecting and Research*. Greenwich, Conn.: New York Graphic Society, 1975.

——. *Work and Worship: The Economic Order of the Shakers*. Greenwich, Conn.: New York Graphic Society, 1974.

Beale, Galen, and Mary Rose Boswell. *The Earth Shall Blossom*. Woodstock, Vt.: The Countryman Press, 1991.

Buchanan, Rita. *The Shaker Herb and Garden Book*. Boston: Houghton Mifflin, 1996.

Carr, Frances. *Shaker Your Plate*. Sabbathday Lake, Maine, 1985.

Kremer, Elizabeth. *We Make You Kindly Welcome*. Harrodsburg, Ky.: Pleasant Hill Press, 1970.

Lassiter, William. *Shaker Recipes for Cooks and Homemakers*. New York, N. Y., 1959.

Miller, Amy Bess. *Shaker Herbs, A History and Compendium*. New York: Clarkson Potter, 1976.

Miller, Amy Bess, and Persis Fuller. *The Best of Shaker Cooking*. New York: Macmillan, 1985.

Miller, M. Stephen. *Marketing Community Industries 1850–1930: A Century of Shaker Ephemera*. New Britain, Conn.: M. Stephen Miller, 1989.

Paige, Jeffrey S. *The Shaker Kitchen*. New York: Clarkson Potter, 1987.

A Guide to Shaker Collections

Shaker Museum,
Sabbathday Lake
Poland Spring, Maine
(207) 926-4597

Shelburne Museum
Shelburne, Vermont
(802) 985-3344

Canterbury Shaker Village
Canterbury, New Hampshire
(603) 783-9511

The Museum at Lower
Shaker Village
Enfield, New Hampshire
(603) 632-4346

Fruitlands Museum,
Prospect Hill
Harvard, Massachusetts
(508) 456-3924

Hancock Shaker Village
Pittsfield, Massachusetts
(413) 443-0188

The Shaker Museum and
Library
Old Chatham, New York
(518) 794-9100

Shaker Historical
Society Museum
Shaker Heights, Ohio
(216) 921-1201

Western Reserve Historical
Society Museum
Cleveland, Ohio
(216) 721-5727

Shaker Village of Pleasant Hill
Harrodsburg, Kentucky
(606) 734-5411

Kentucky Museum
Bowling Green, Kentucky
(502) 745-2592

Shakertown at South Union
South Union, Kentucky
(502) 542-4167

Notes on the Photographs and Artwork

The following locations appear in Paul Rocheleau's photographs: Canterbury Shaker Village, Canterbury, New Hampshire, images appear on pages 8, 33, 48, 68, and 85; Shaker Village of Pleasant Hill, Harrodsburg, Kentucky, images appear on pages 12, 18, 21, 26, 28, 31, 36, 43, 51, 61, 62, 65, 75, 77, 81, and 87; Lebanon Shaker Village, Mt. Lebanon, New York, images appear on pages 17, 23, 35, and 38; The Museum of Lower Shaker Village, Enfield, New Hampshire, images appear on the jacket cover and on pages 41, 55, and 73.

The Shaker Seed Company poster appearing on page ii is courtesy of the New York State Museum, Albany, New York.

The photograph of the spirit drawing appearing on page vi is attributed to Polly Collins and is courtesy of The Library of Congress.

Map of Canterbury Shaker Village by Henry Blinn appearing on the endpapers and on page 14 is courtesy of Canterbury Shaker Village, Canterbury, New Hampshire.

The Wreath of Roses spirit drawing appearing on page 59 is courtesy of The Western Reserve Historical Society, Cleveland, Ohio.

The following images are from the Collection of M. Stephen and Miriam R. Miller: cabbage seed package on page 24; Seven Barks label on page 44; Tamar Laxative on page 52; Shaker Medicinal Spring Water advertisement on page 56; Shaker Apple Sauce and Fresh Apples labels on page 67; and the sweet corn label on page 82.

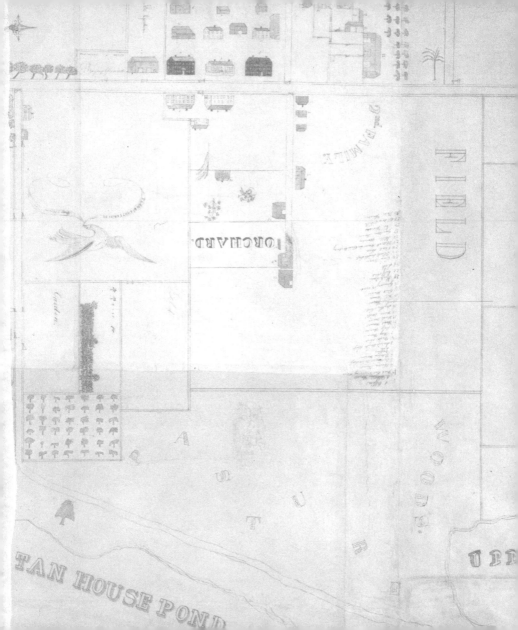

FIELD

Genl FAMILY

ORCHARD

WOODS

Garden.

PASTURE

TAN HOUSE POND

PAST

Meadow

FIELD.

FIELD.

Pasture.

FIELD.

FIELD.

Meeting House

FIELD.

FIELD.

VEGETABLE GARDEN

TAN HOUSE FIELD.

S. MILL FIELD.

S. M. POND.

TURNING

MILL

POND.